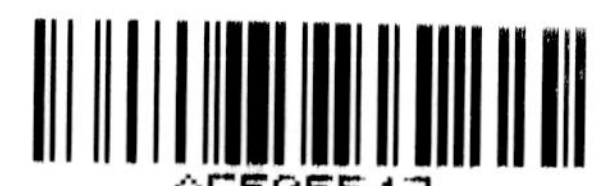
AF505547

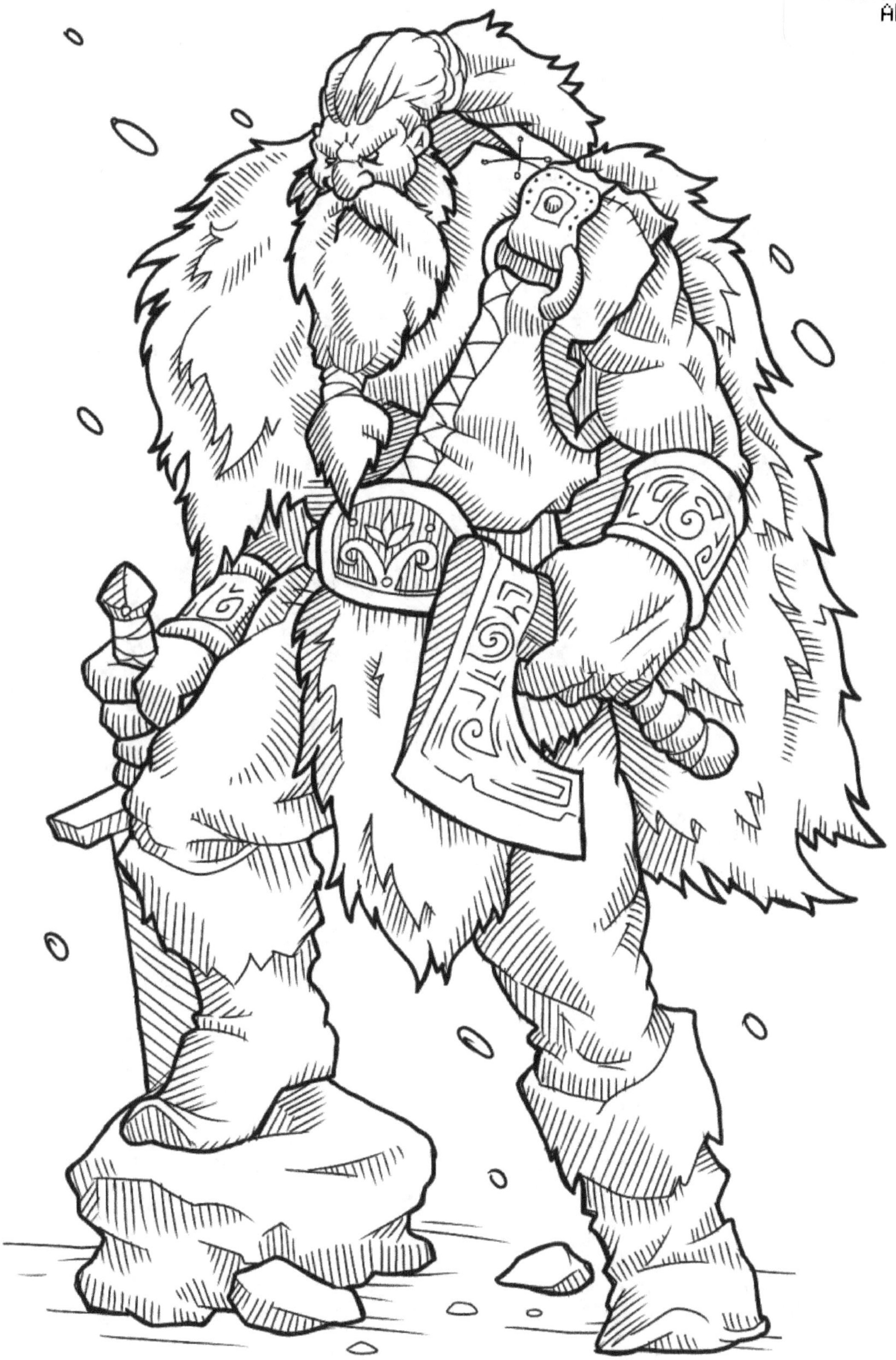

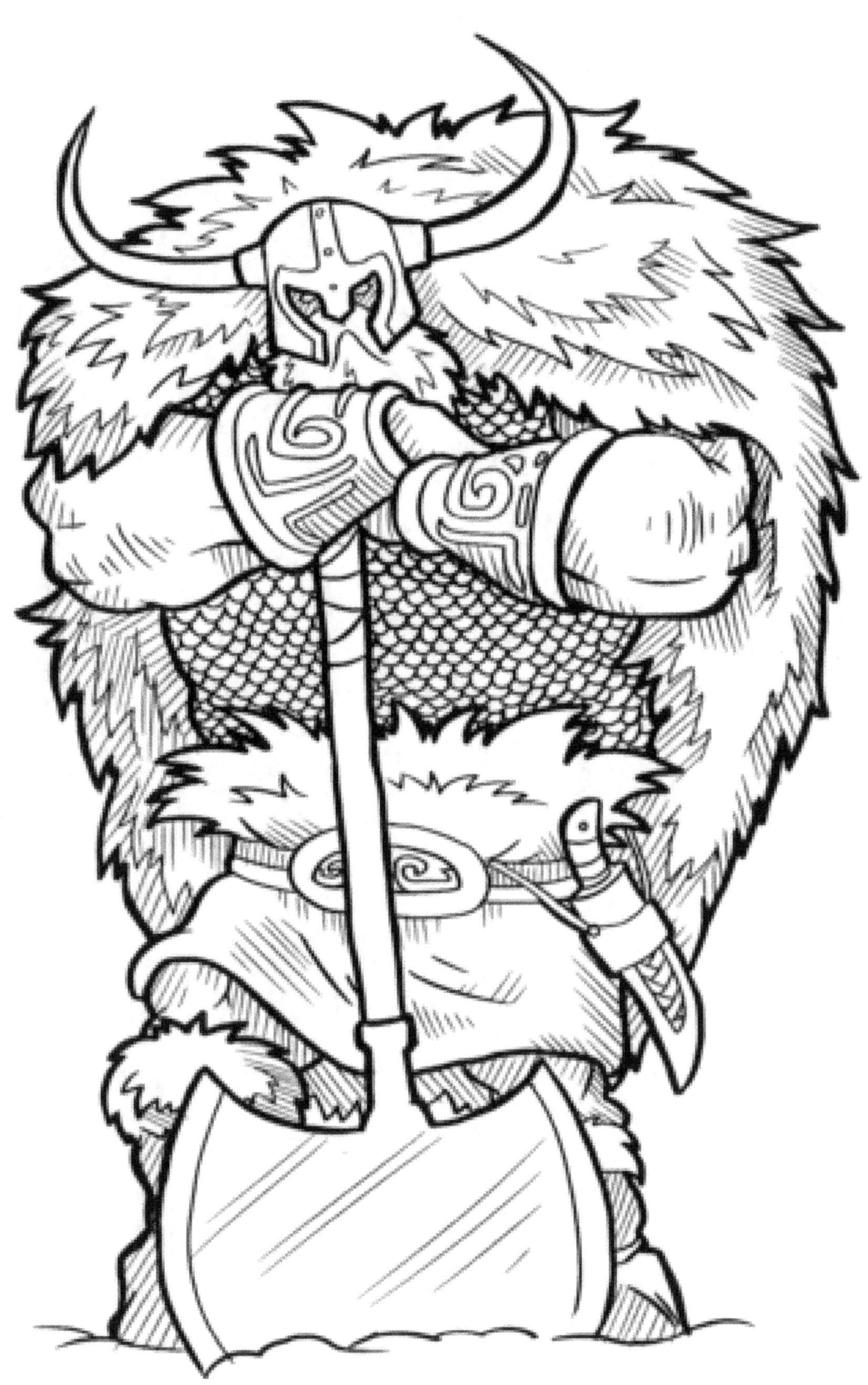

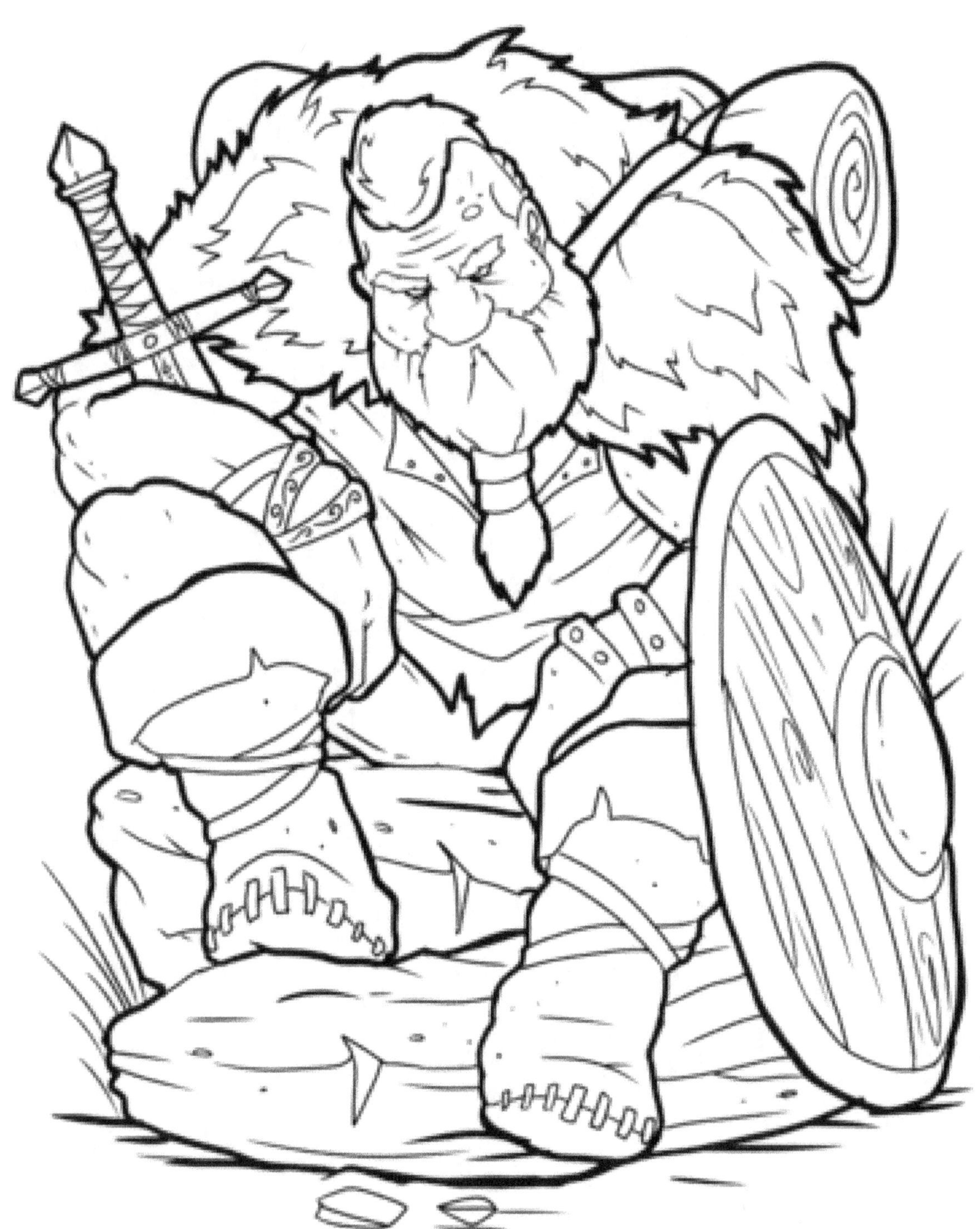

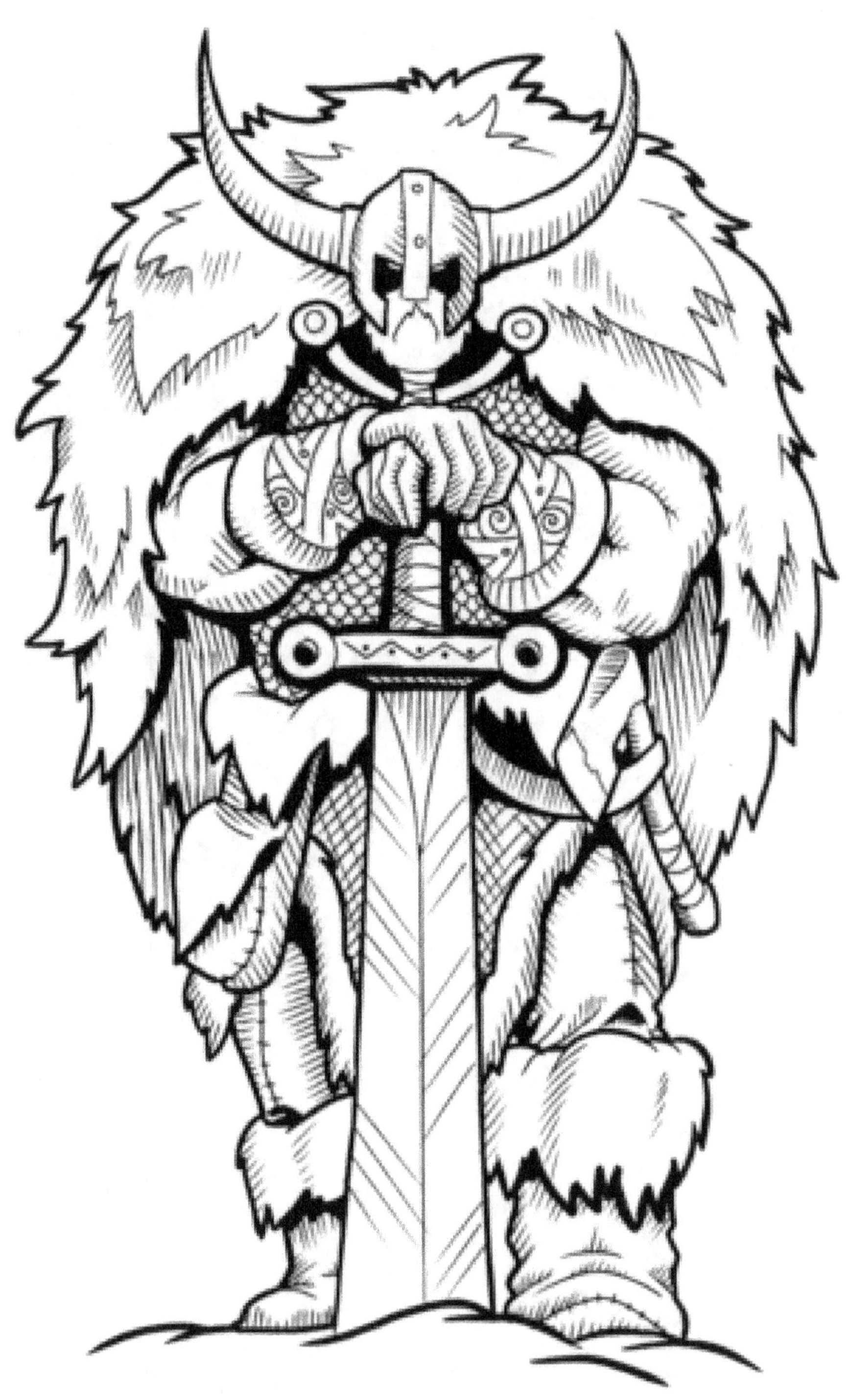

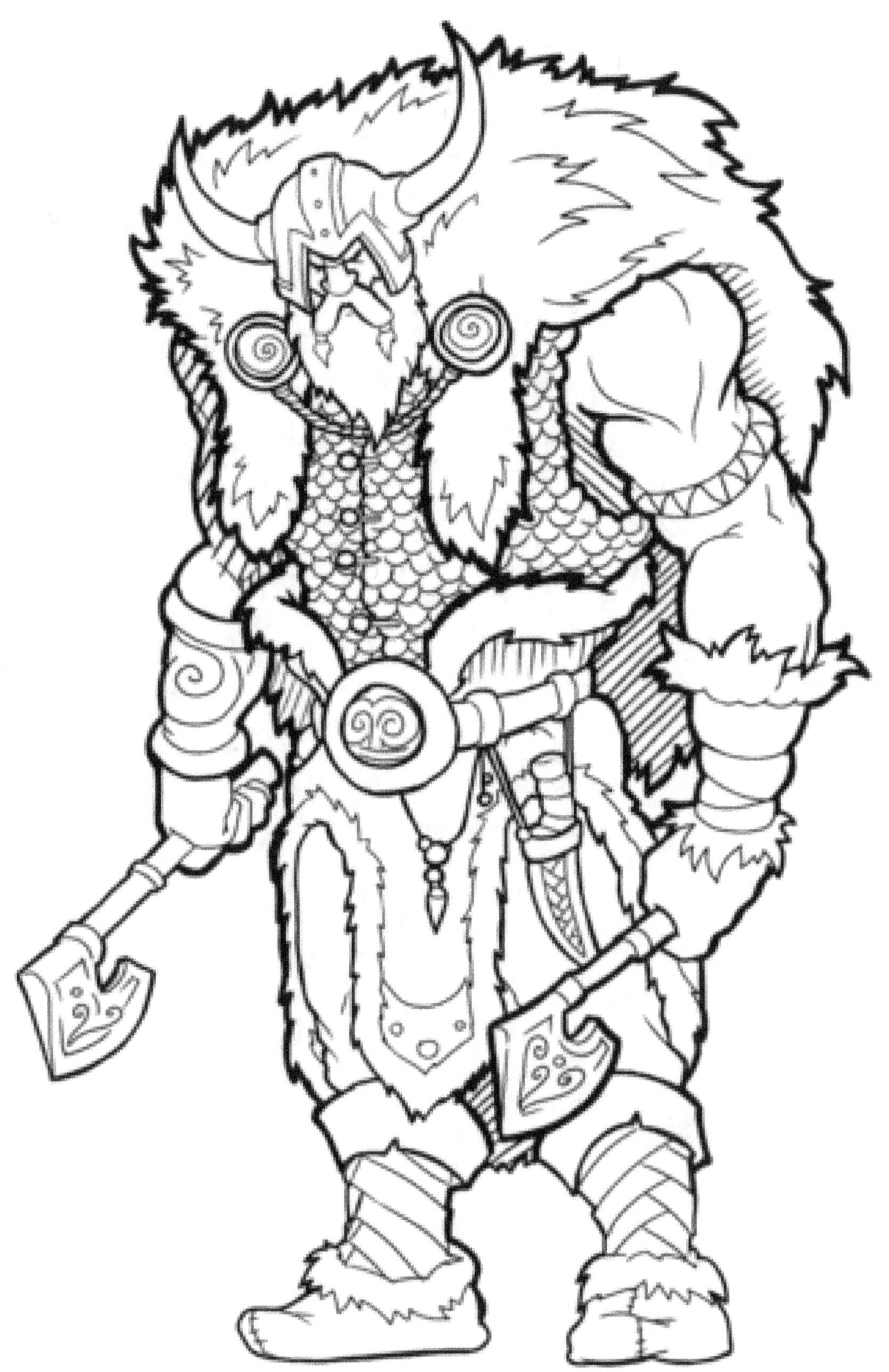

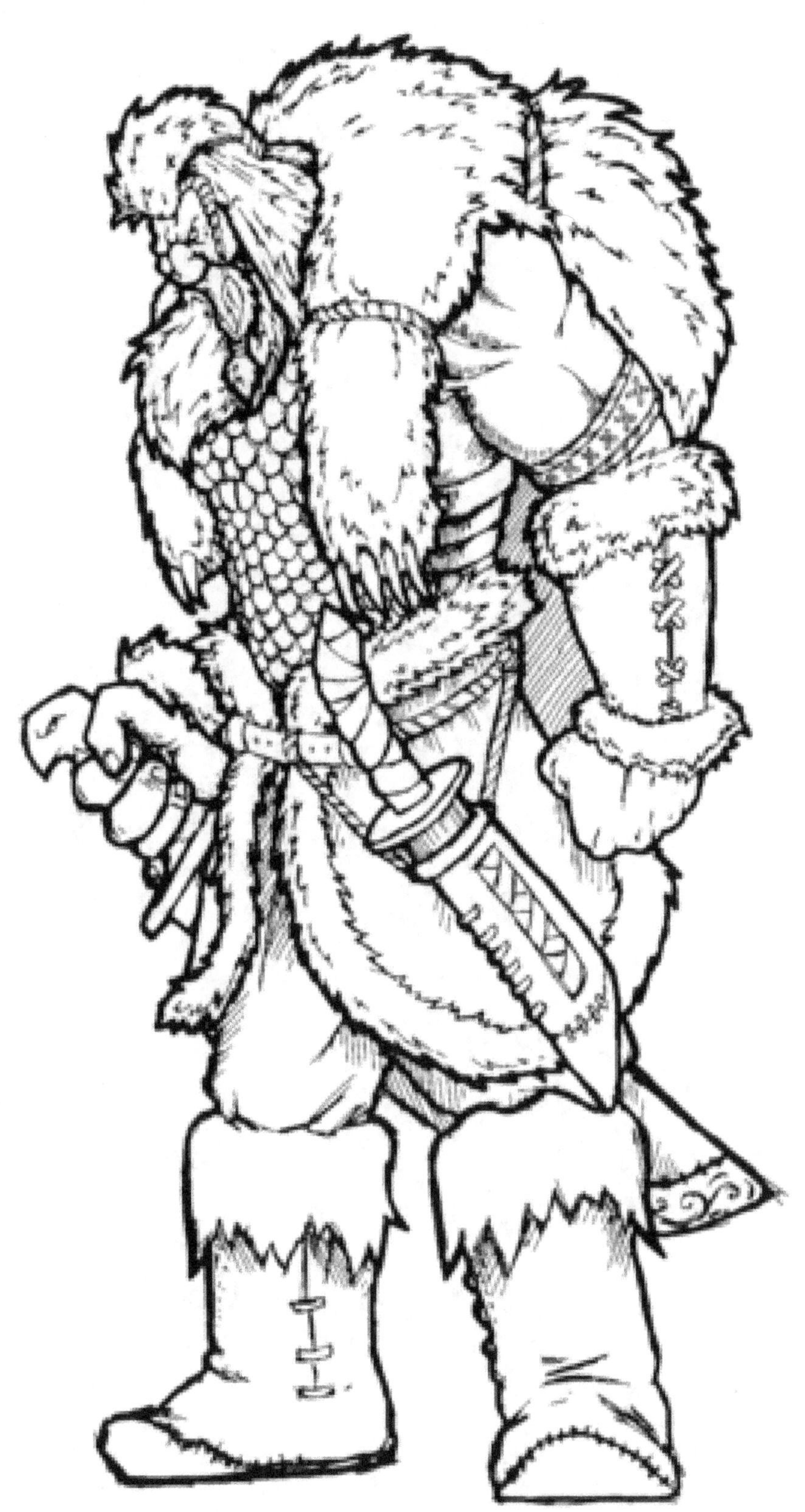

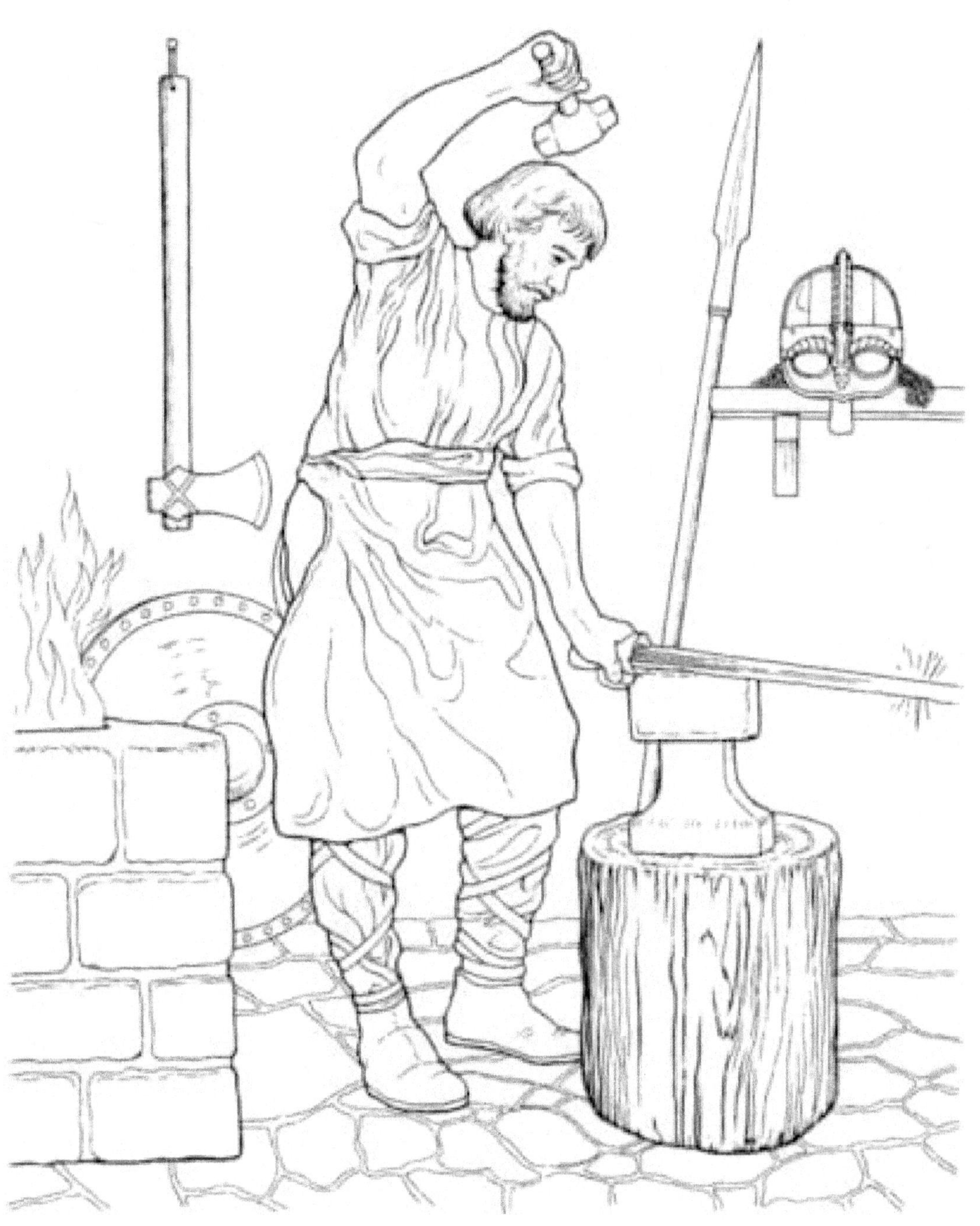

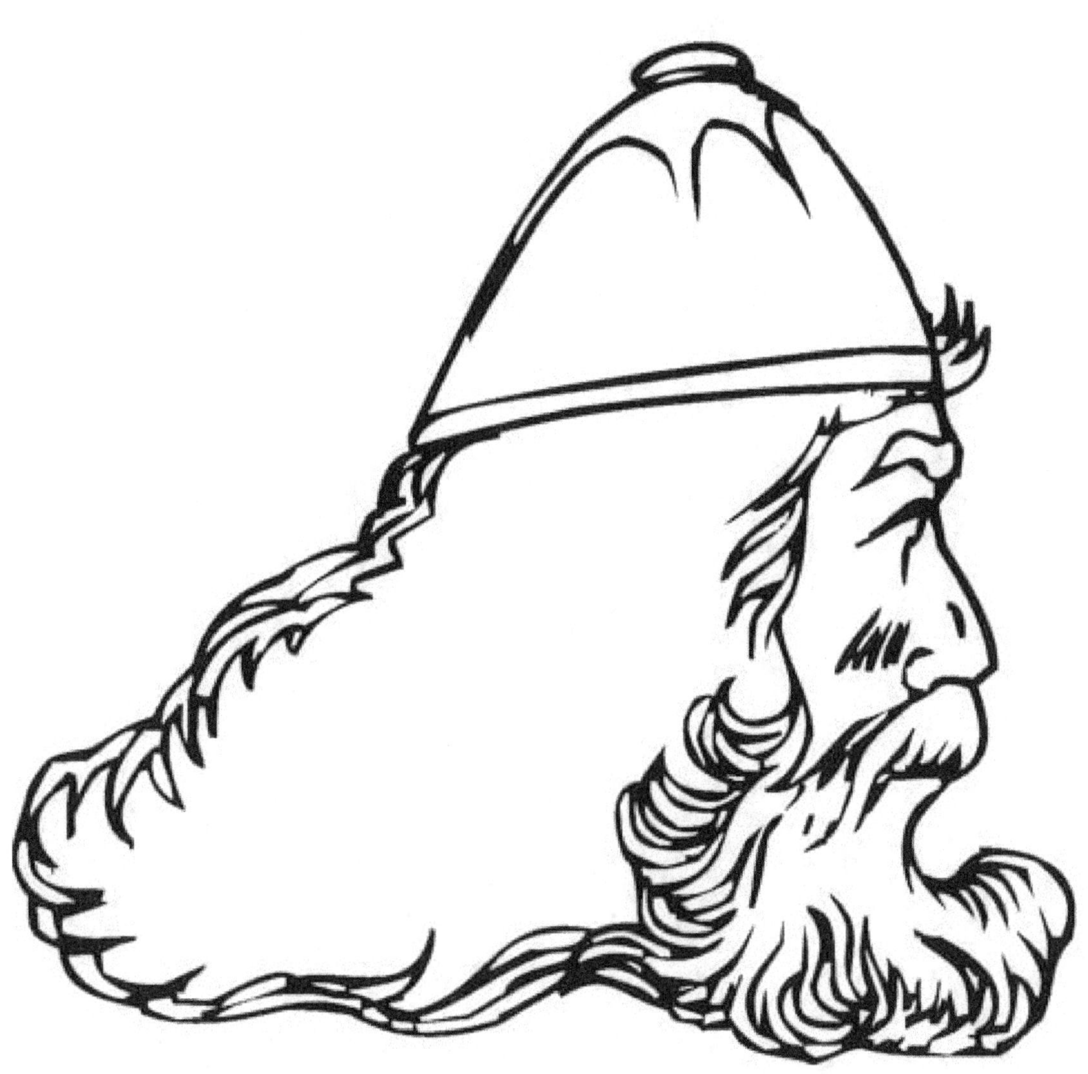

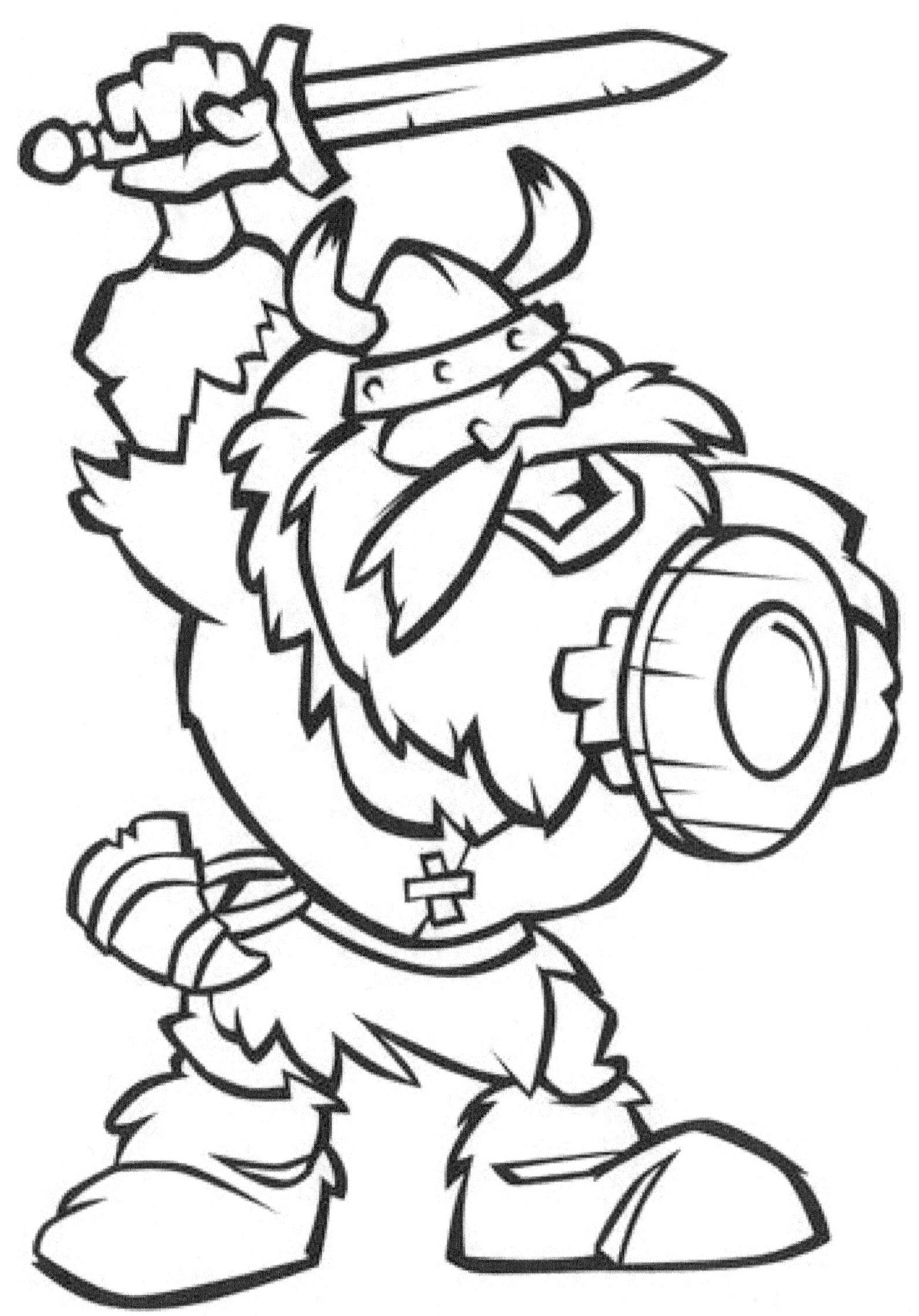

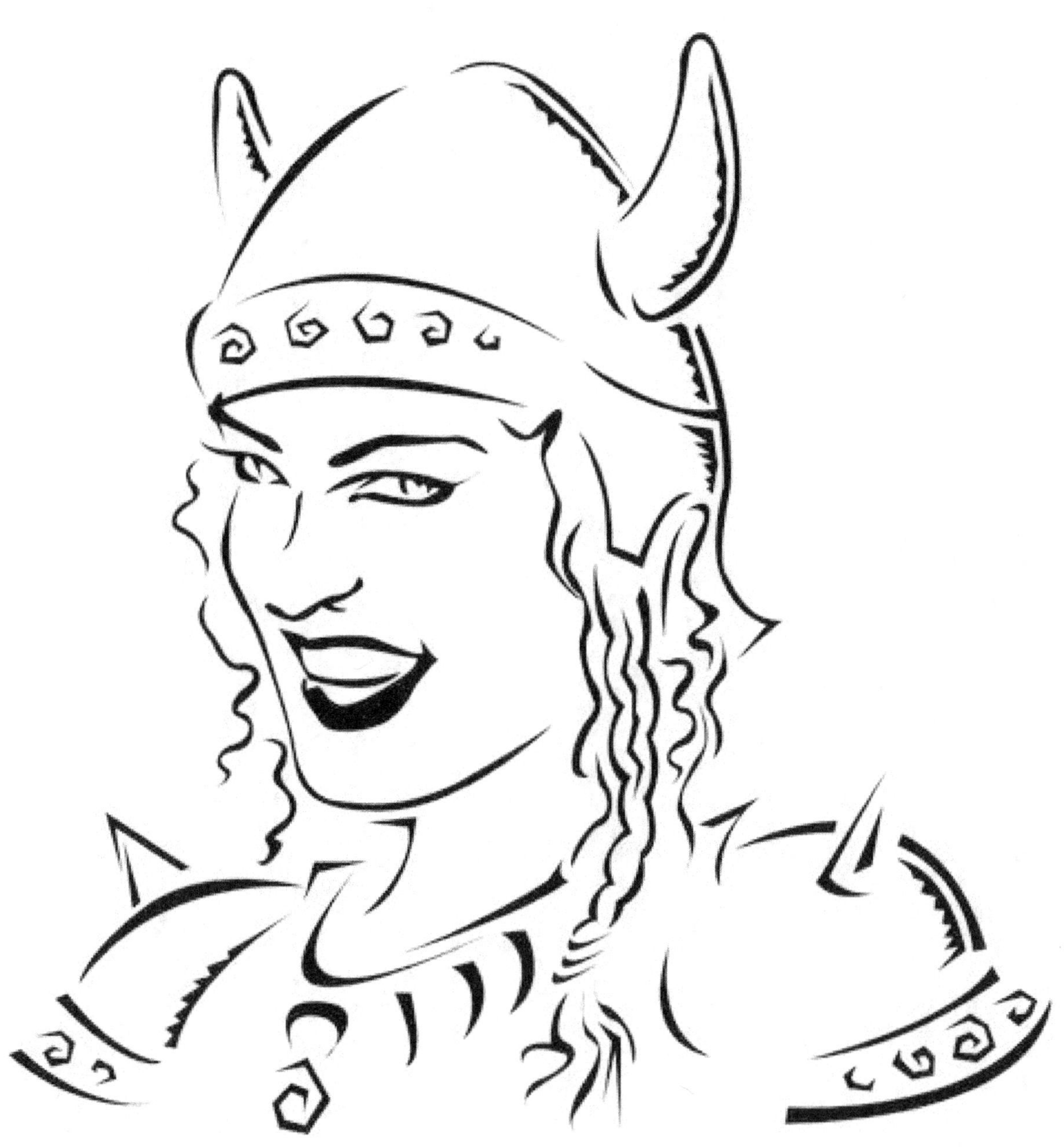

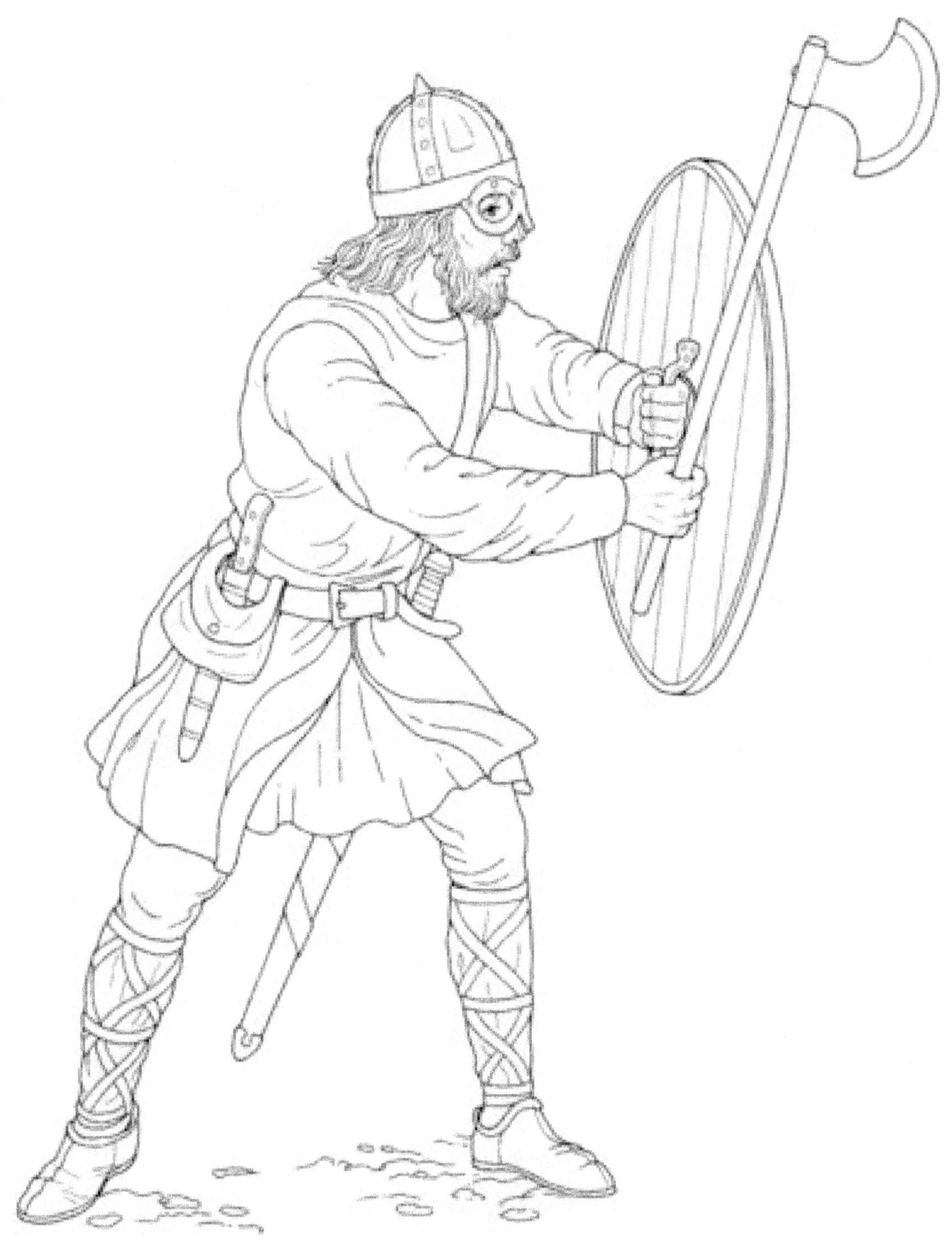

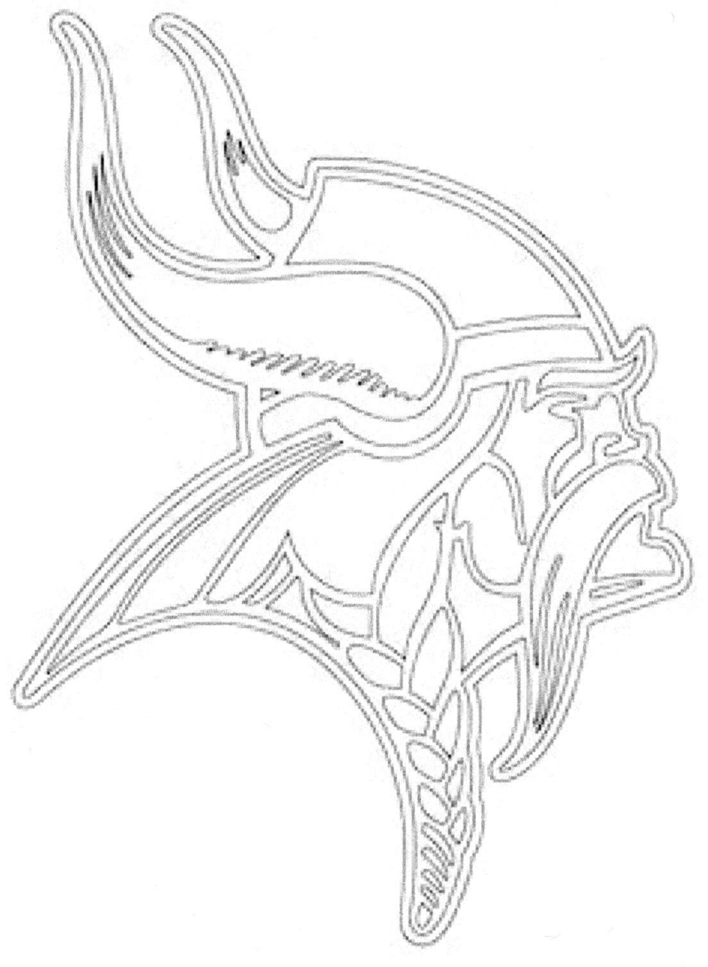

VIKINGS

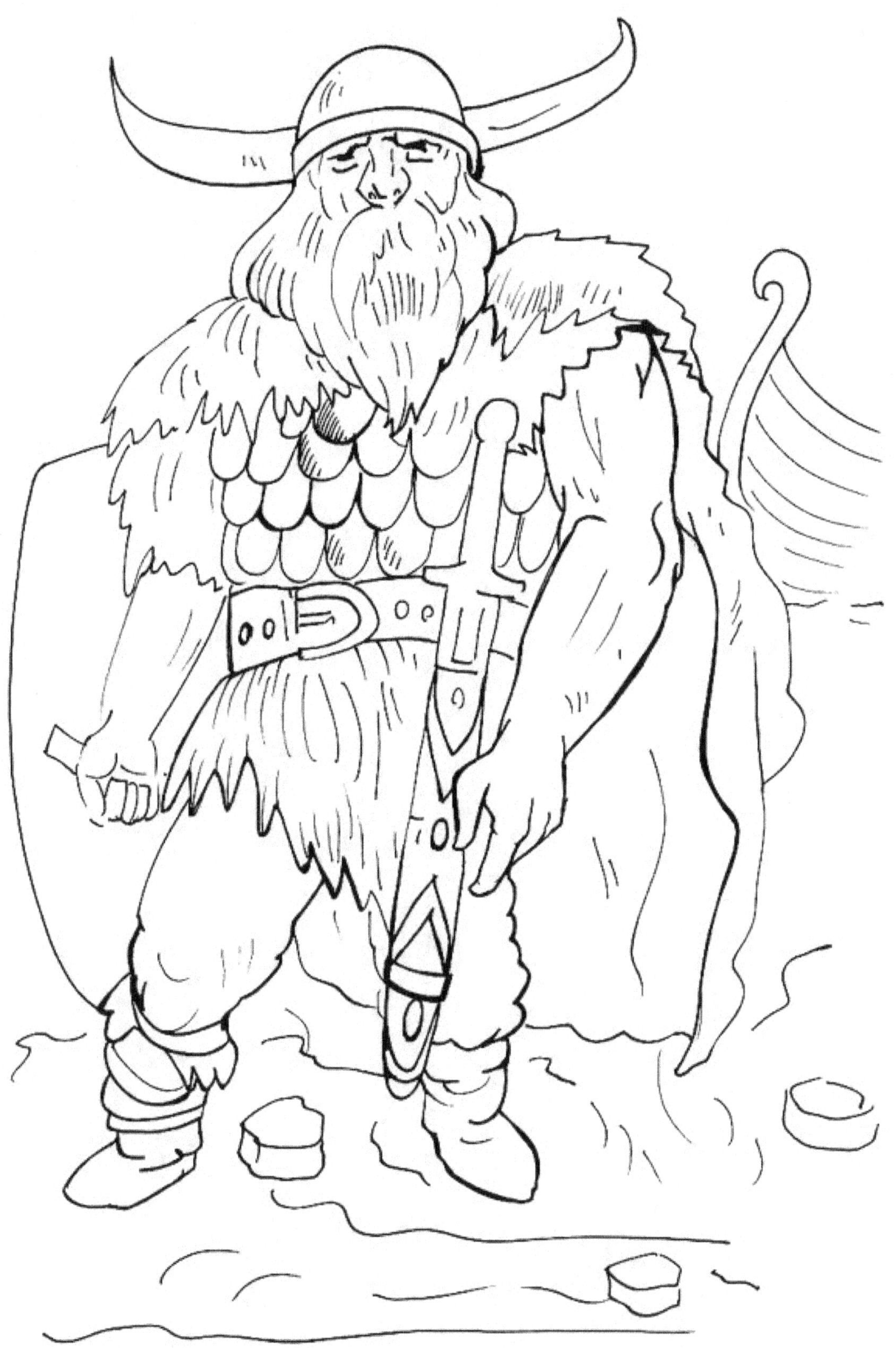

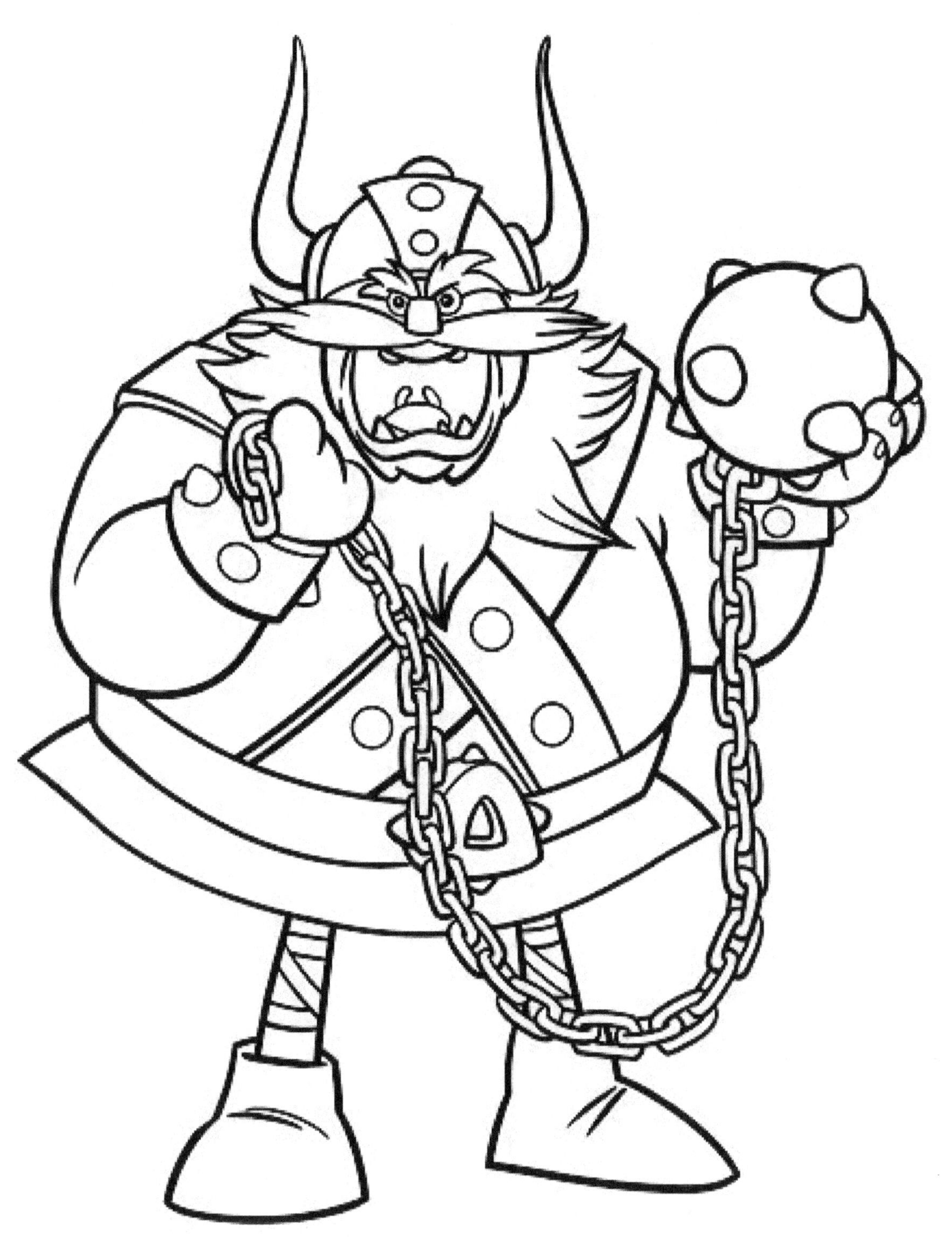

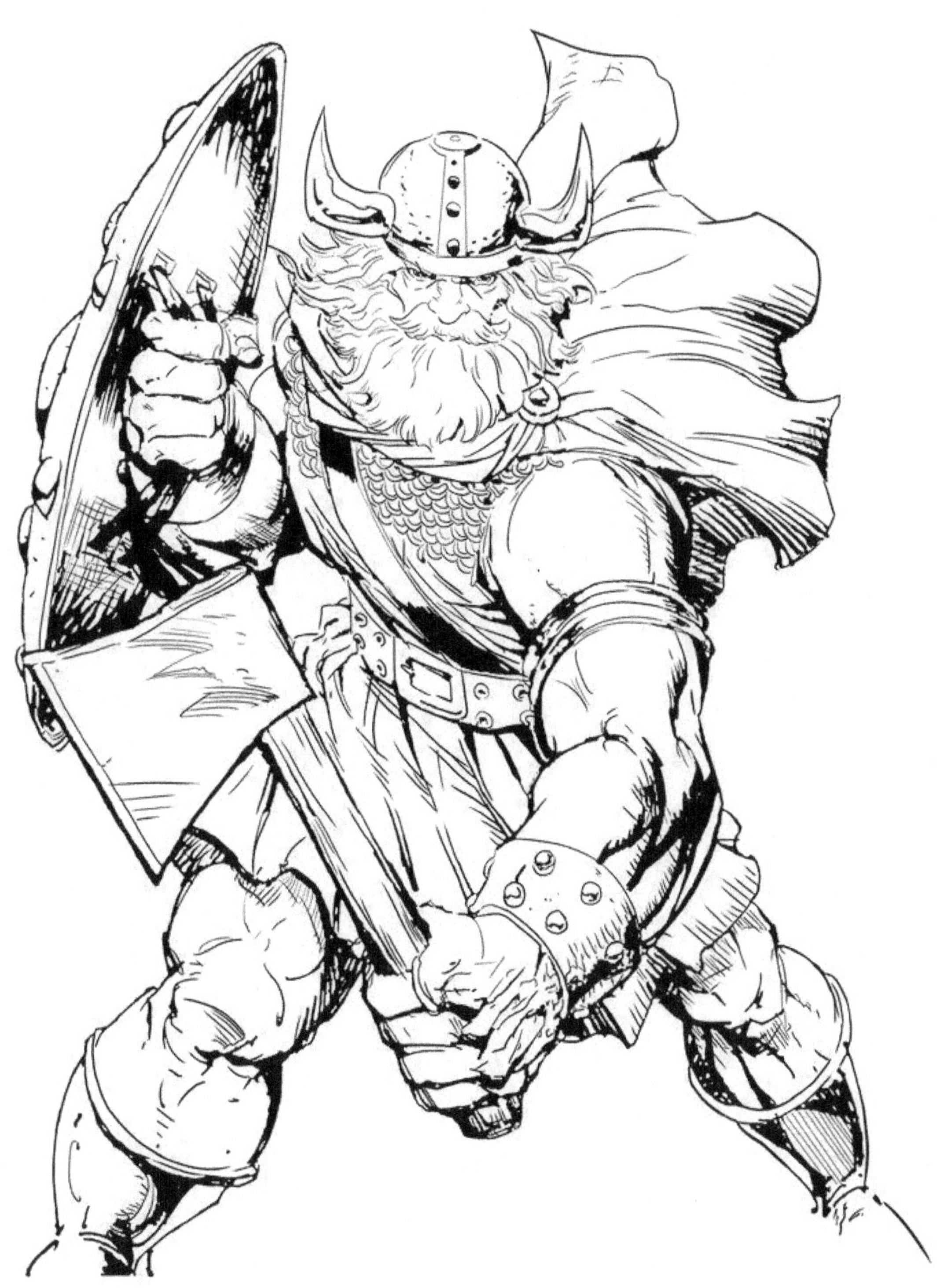

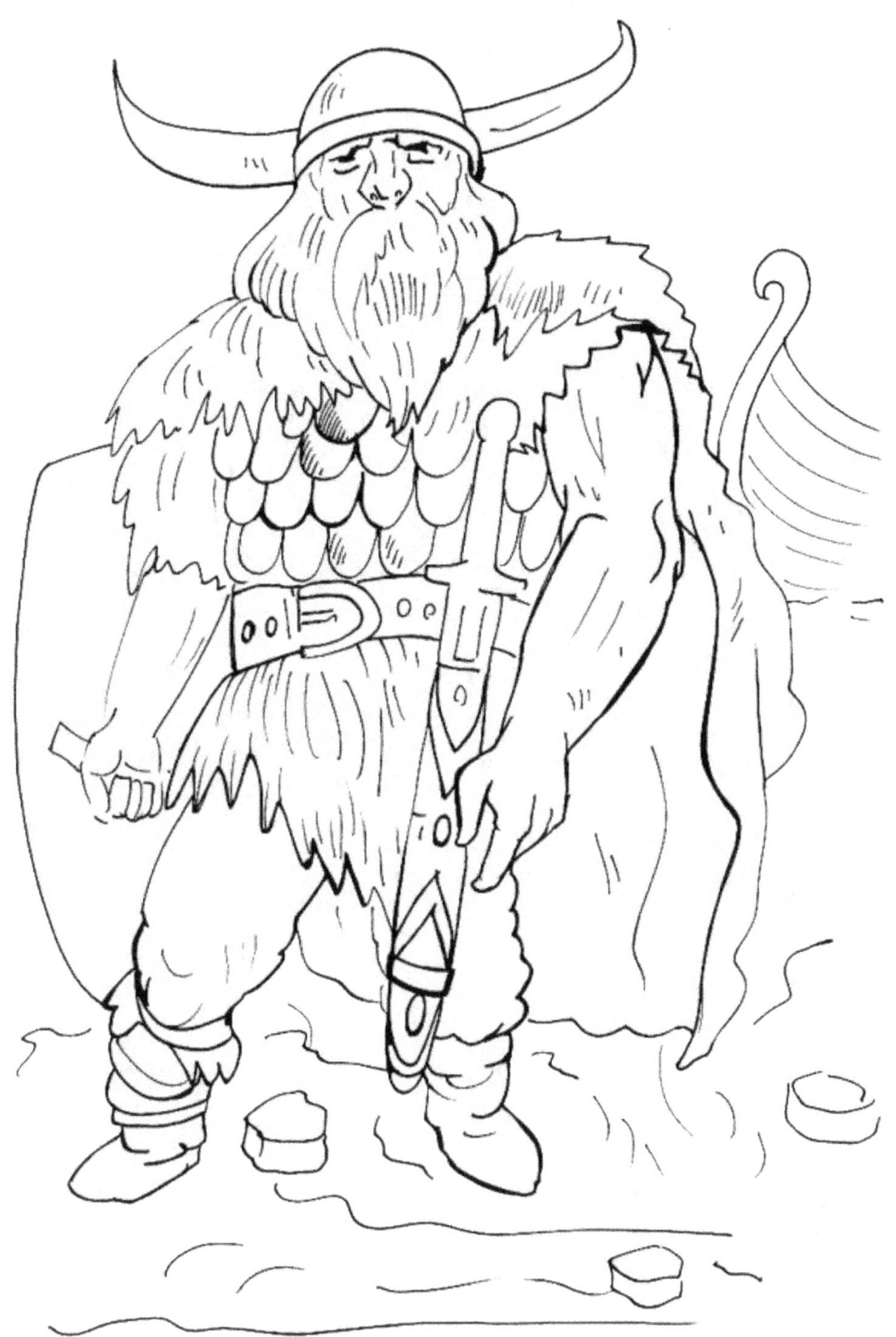

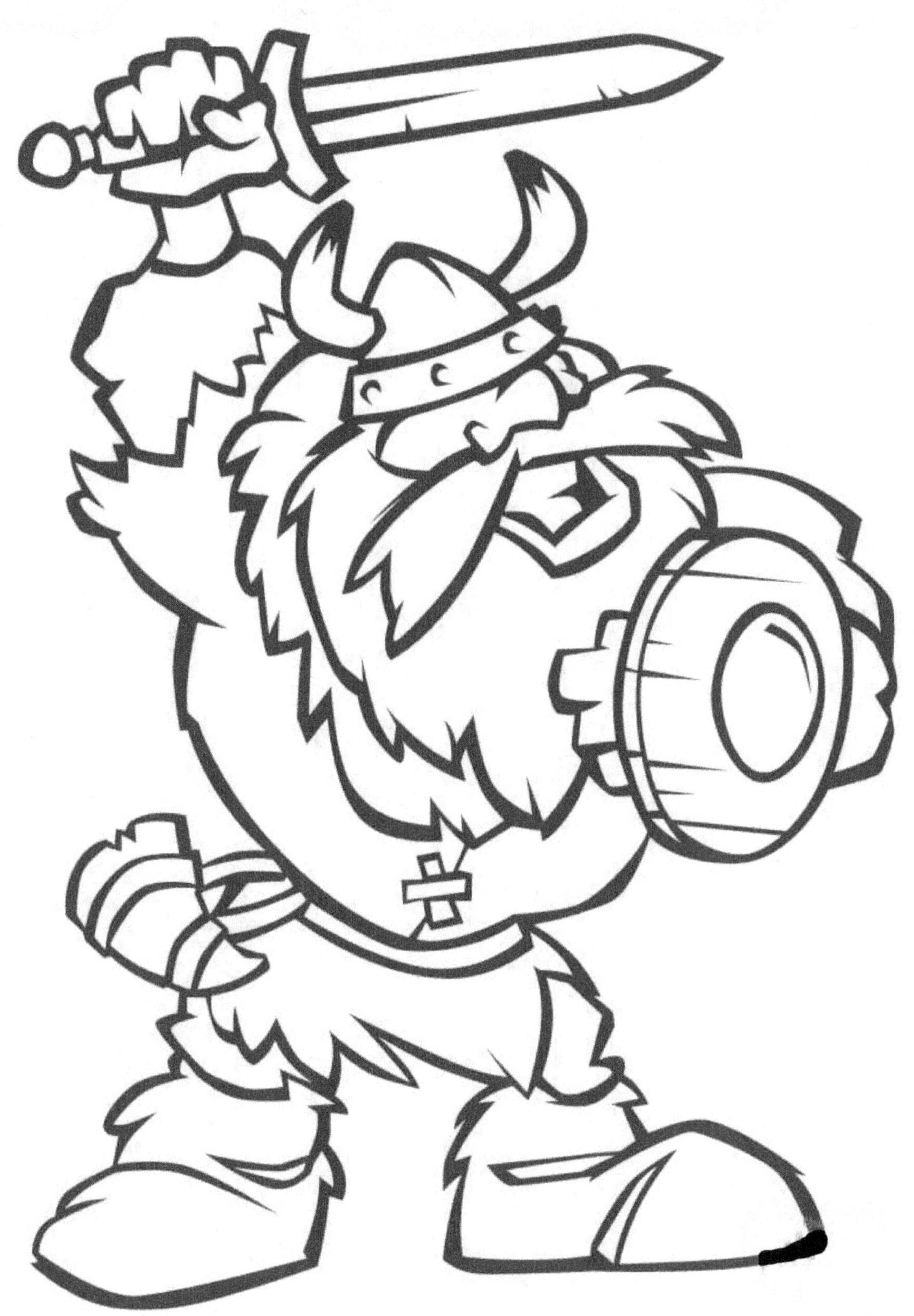

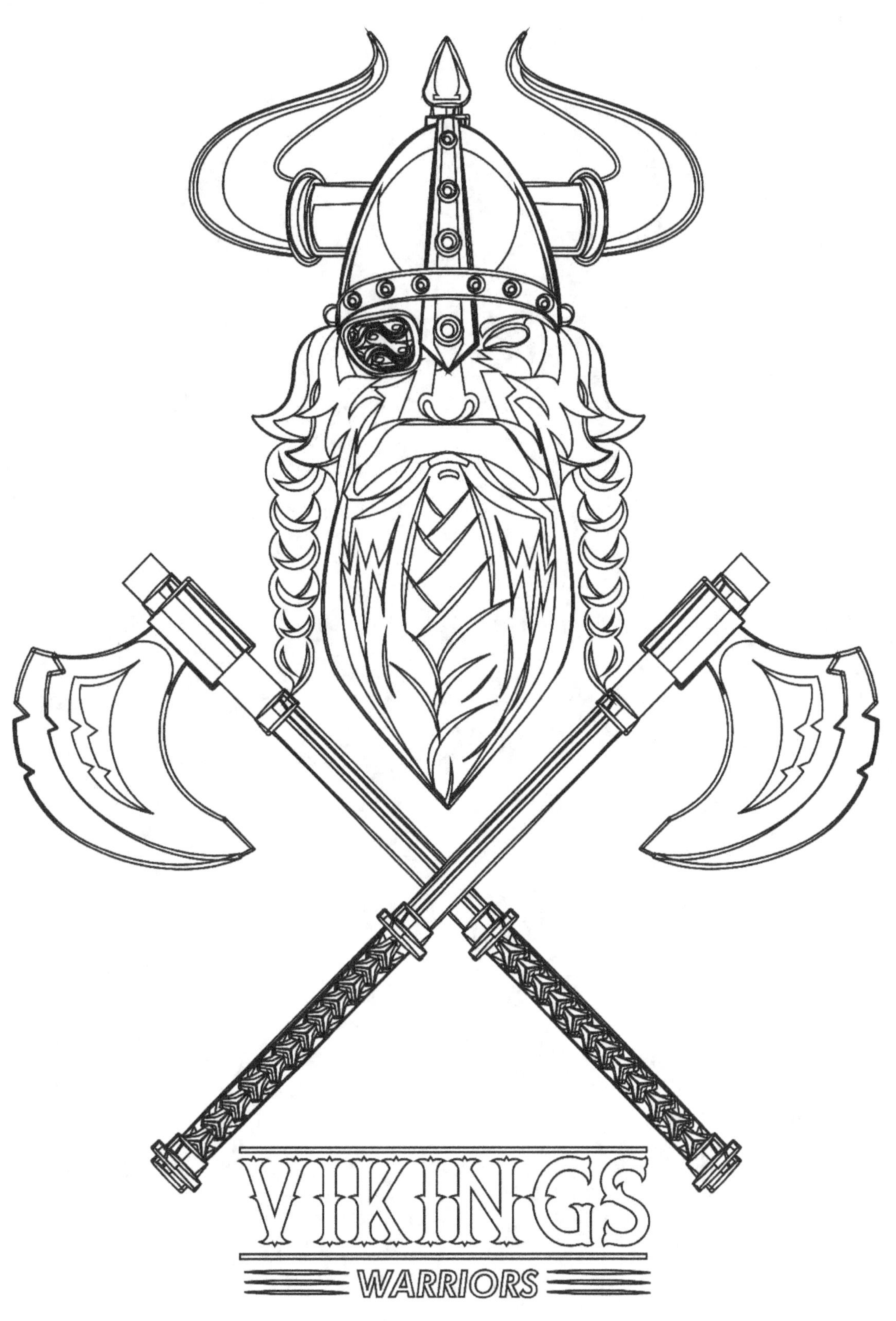

VIKINGS
WARRIORS

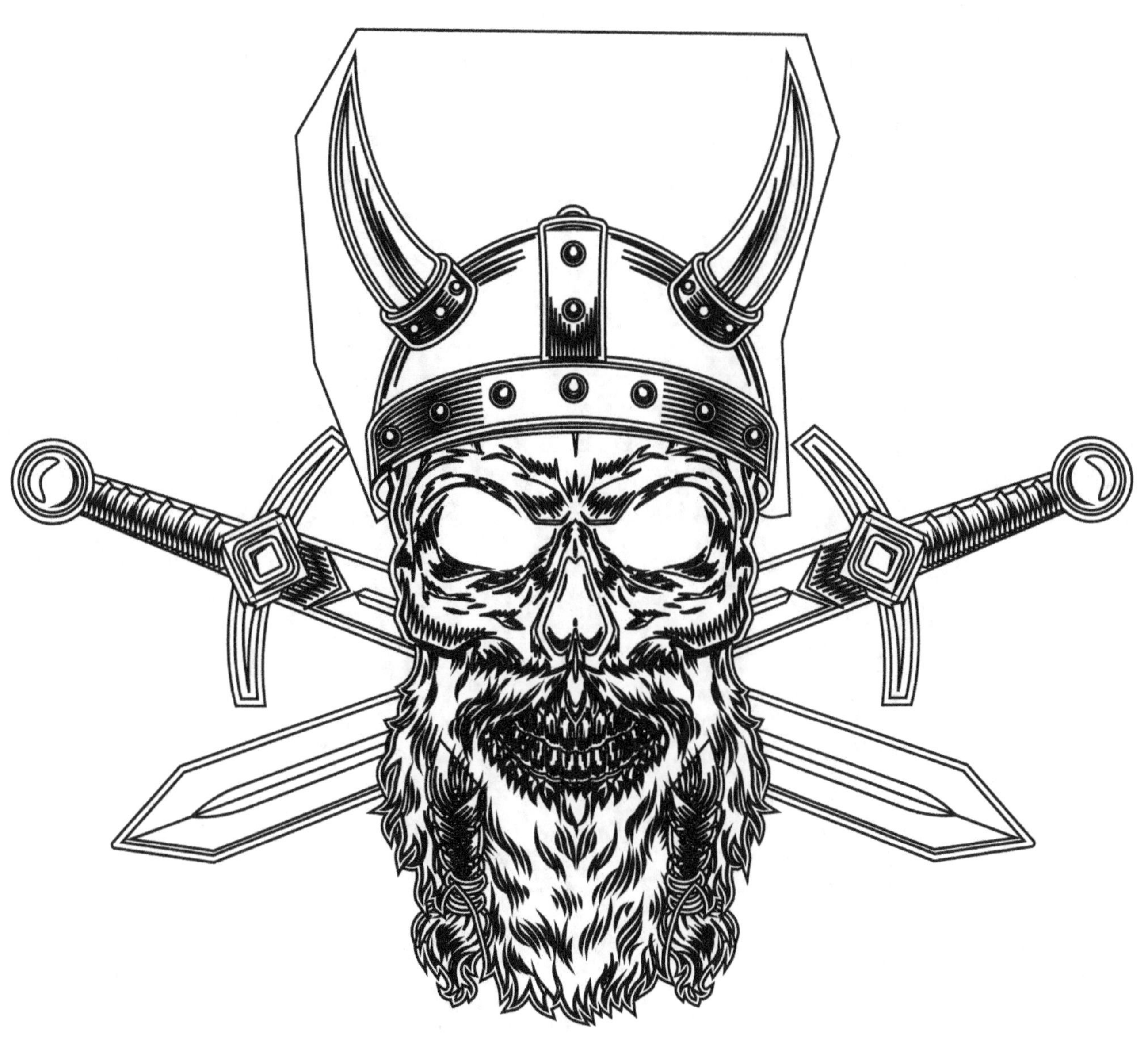

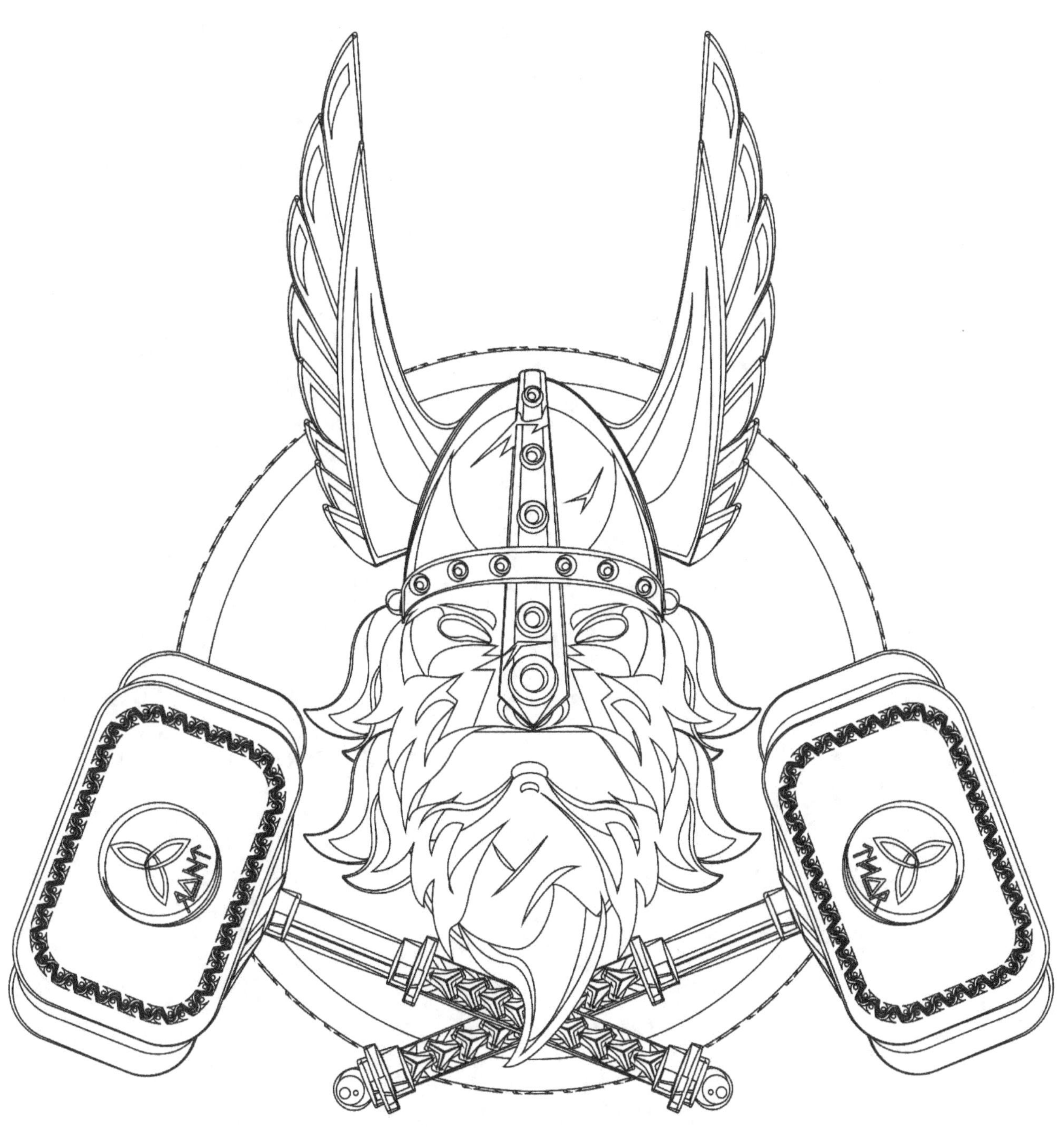
RANT
THOR
VIKINGS
THOR

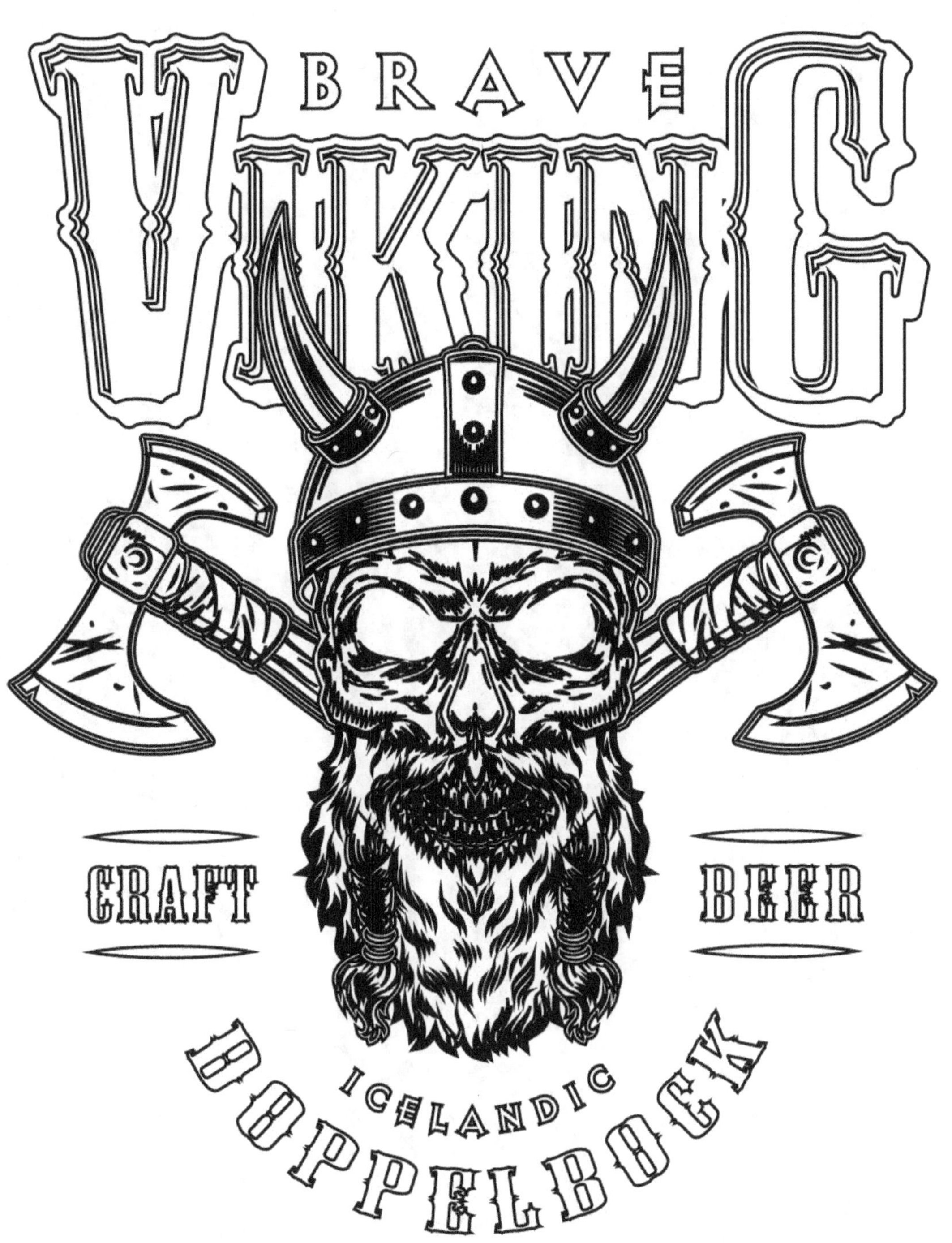

BRAVE
VIKING
CRAFT
BEER
ICELANDIC
DOPPELBOCK

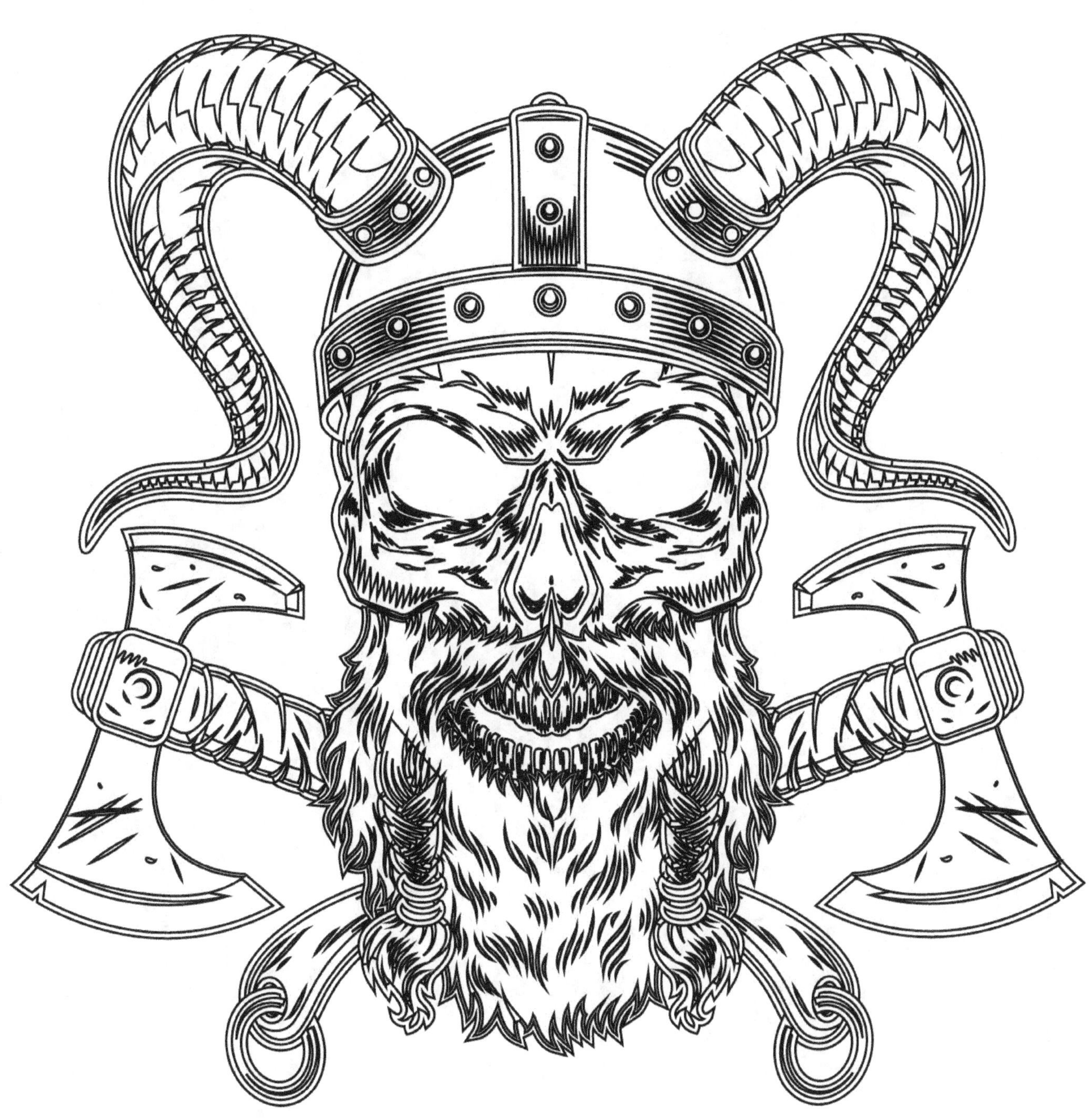

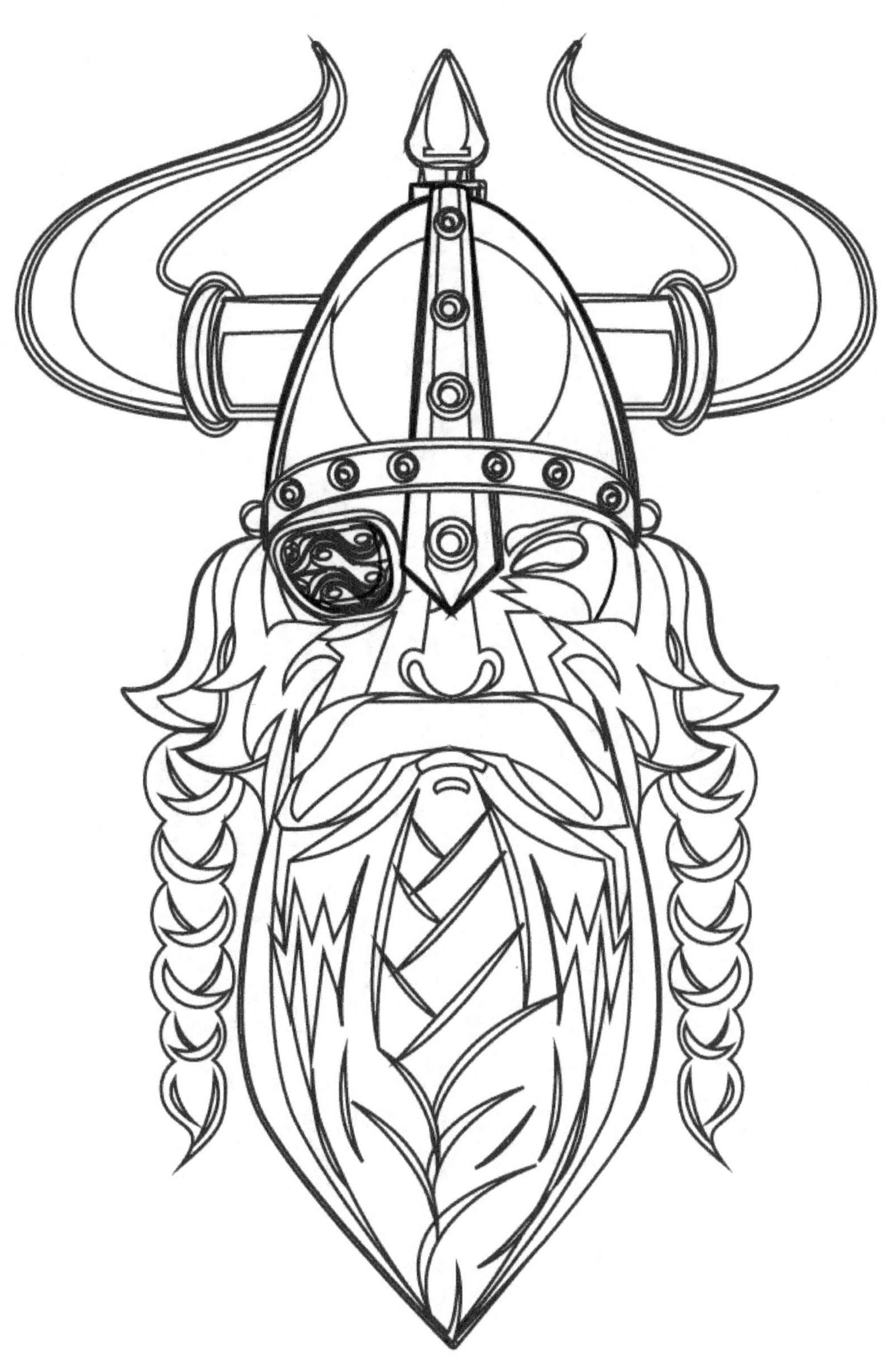

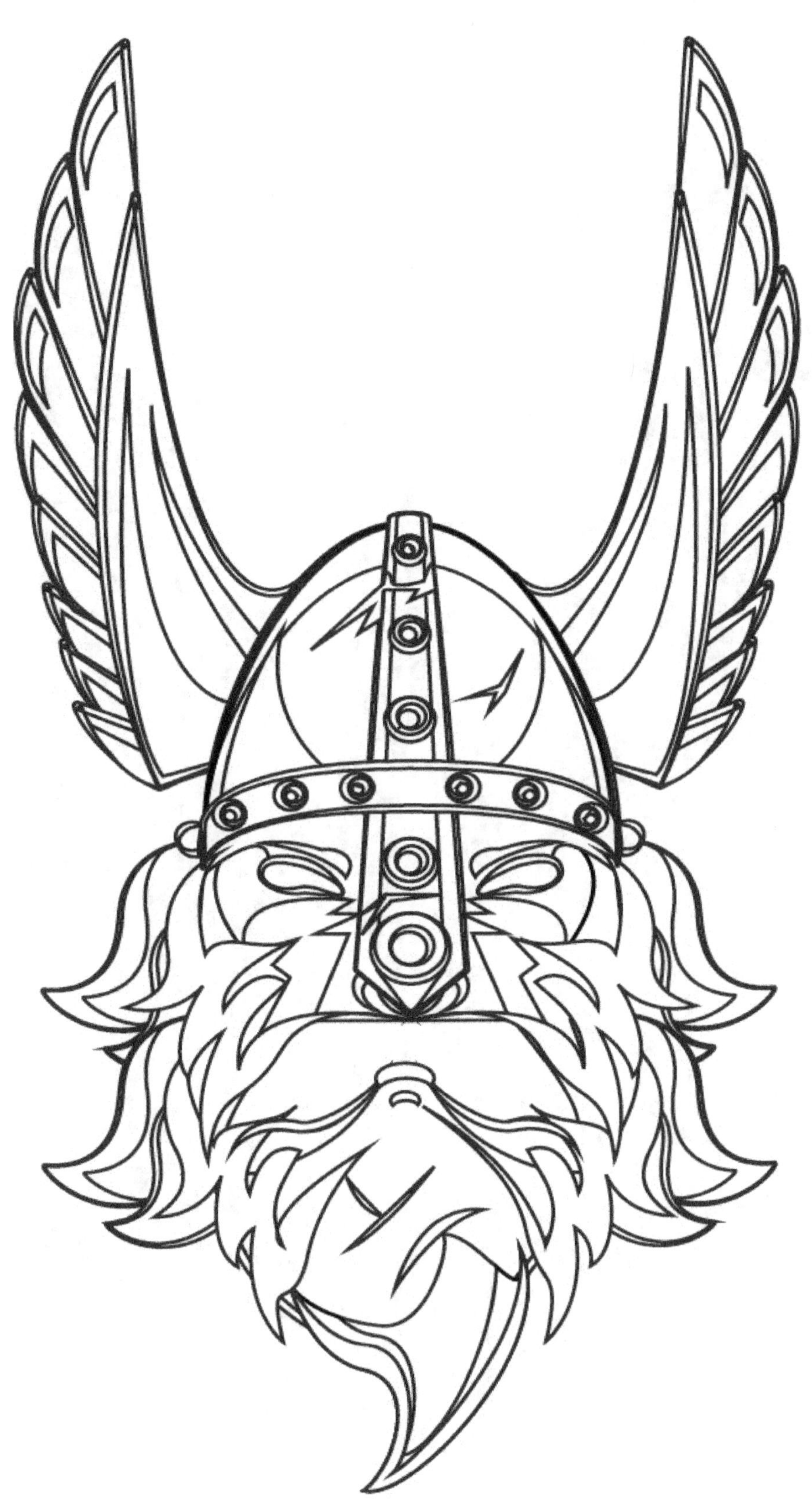

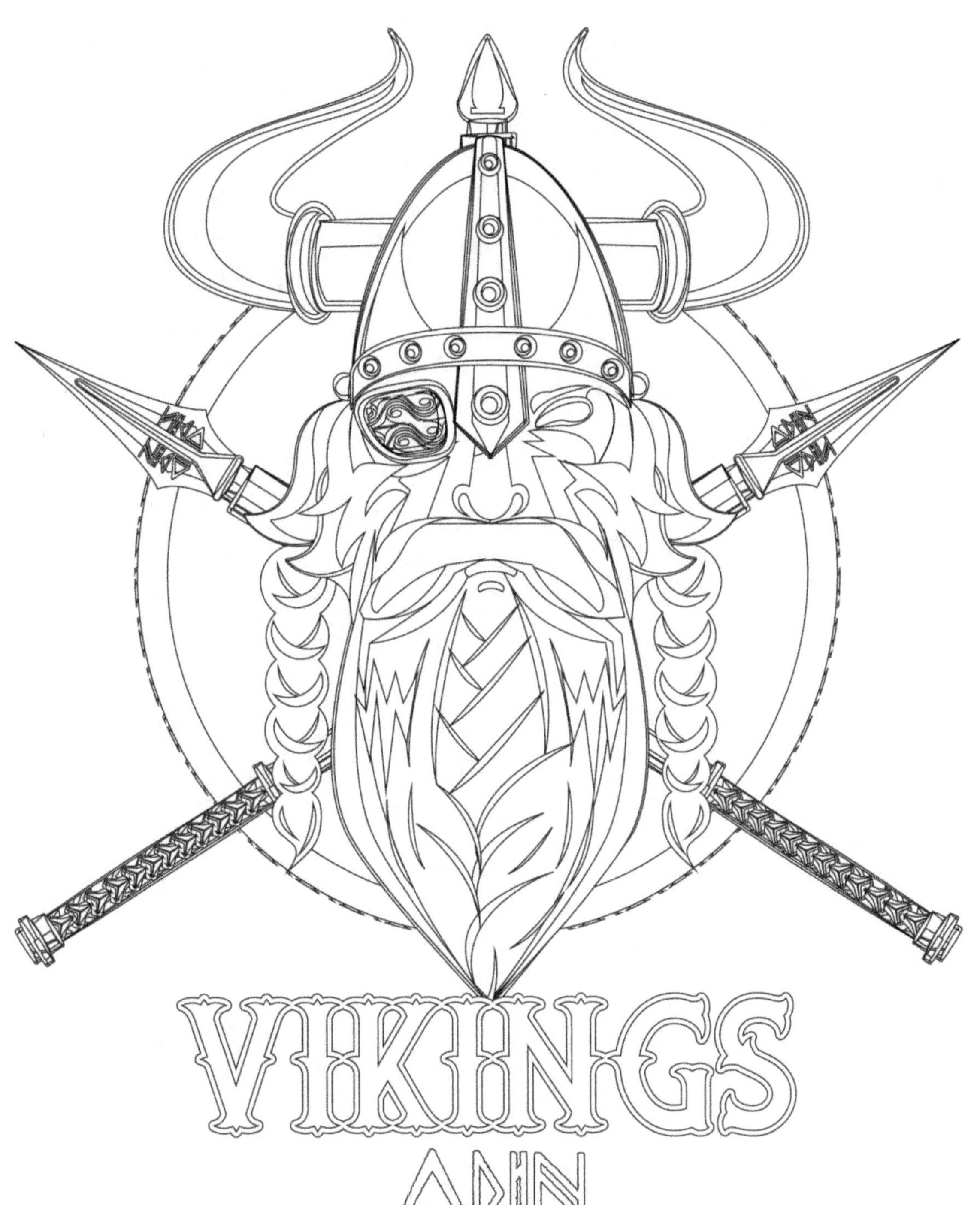

VIKINGS
ODIN